IMAGES
of America

CHILLICOTHE

OHIO

Pictured on the Ross County Courthouse steps in 1895 are two baseball teams, dubbed the Fats and the Leans, and the Londonderry Band. A.T. Swepston and Mayor Charles Waddle organized the game as a fund-raiser for the city hospital, which was then in a house on Bridge Street. Players on the Fats team weighed over 200 pounds, and those on the Leans under 200 pounds. Waddle, armed with a pistol and a saber, umpired, and the band provided entertainment. In the game, played in City Park, the Leans beat the Fats.

IMAGES
of America

CHILLICOTHE
OHIO

G. Richard Peck

ARCADIA
PUBLISHING

Published by Arcadia Publishing
Charleston, South Carolina

Library of Congress Catalog Card Number: 2001086406

For all general information contact Arcadia Publishing at:
Telephone 843-853-2070
Fax 843-853-0044
E-mail sales@arcadiapublishing.com
For customer service and orders:
Toll-Free 1-888-313-2665

Visit us on the Internet at www.arcadiapublishing.com

This is the table on which Ohio's first constitution was signed by members of the Constitutional Convention in 1802. It is on display at the Ross County Historical Society, 45 West Fifth Street, Chillicothe.

On the Cover: The Ohio and Erie Canal came through Chillicothe in 1831. This footbridge over the canal at the head of Walnut Street was built in 1893.

CONTENTS

The seal for the city of Chillicothe was designed by H.H. Bennett. Self-government for Chillicothe began in 1802, and by 1838, the city was incorporated.

INTRODUCTION

The city of Chillicothe is located in south-central Ohio, some 45 miles south of the state capital of Columbus and 45 miles north of Portsmouth on the Ohio River. This is where the flatlands of central Ohio meet the foothills of the Appalachians. The story of how this area of Ohio was settled is quite interesting.

After failed attempts to found a colony in the New World, King James I of England wrote the 1609 charter for the founding of the colony of Virginia. Thinking that part of the reason for previous failures was too small a land area, he specified dimensions that had Virginia extending across the entire continent. After the Revolutionary War when Virginia was one of the original 13 states, she used this 1609 charter to claim huge areas of land to the west. In order to help get the smaller states to ratify the Constitution, Virginia gave up most of her claims except for a couple of areas, the largest being in "The Territory of the United States northwest of the river Ohio."[1] Some 4.2 million acres between the Little Miami and Scioto Rivers, and extending as far north as Kenton, was retained by Virginia as land to be given to the soldiers who fought against England during the Revolutionary War. Coincident with the Ordinance of 1787, which defined the territory, Virginia held the area exempt from federal control until the land warrants could be distributed to the soldiers and their descendants. The area became known as the Virginia Military District. It took until 1790 for the land warrants to be awarded, and most of them ended up being sold to anyone interested in moving to the wilderness.

In 1783, coincident with Virginia giving up other major land claims, a 17 year old named Nathaniel Massie set off from Virginia with a land warrant for property located by Daniel Boone in what later became the state of Kentucky. Massie's father had given him the warrant and some money to go and prosper in the West, and prosper he did. He learned the value of locating and surveying land and acquiring the same. In 1790, Massie was appointed deputy surveyor by Col. Richard Clough Anderson, the principal surveyor of the Virginia Military District. Massie and some of his friends and relatives began acquiring huge blocks of land for as little as 5¢ an acre. Also in 1790, Massie founded a settlement on the north side of the Ohio River, which is now Manchester. It was from this place that he conducted a series of land-location and surveying treks throughout the Virginia Military District.

In 1793, Massie discovered an area of land between the Scioto River and Paint Creek. There, hills to the west afforded protection, and land to the east was level and rich, to where the two streams met. The river to the north formed a huge horseshoe bend, but the bluff on which Massie stood seemed high enough to offer protection from floods. This is where Massie eventually founded a town. He returned to this site in 1795 during negotiations with the Native Americans for the Treaty of Greenville, but his party encountered some unfriendly Shawnee.

A struggle ensued and some of the Shawnee were killed. Massie and his group went back to Manchester, planning to return the following year.

To entice settlers to come back with him, Massie promised an in-lot and an out-lot if they promised to remain for two years. The settlers came in 1796 and founded Chillicothe, a name based on the Shawnee word *Cheelakawtha*, meaning "town" or "settlement" or "gathering place." By 1798, when the two-year interval lapsed, Massie kept his word by deeding over the lots. The county of Ross was formed also in 1798, with Chillicothe as the county seat, which made the filing and recording of deeds easier. Many of these original deeds are still on file at the Ross County Courthouse.

As word got out about a new settlement and available land, more Virginians and Kentuckians came. They were intelligent people, eager to build a new state. This concept was opposed to the view held by territorial Gov. Arthur St. Clair, and a political squabble ensued. Finally, in 1800, the territory was split and Chillicothe became the capital of the eastern part, paving the way for statehood. Ohio was born in Chillicothe in 1803, and Chillicothe became Ohio's first capital.

Papermaking came to the region in 1810 and still exists as one of the area's prime industries. In 1831, the Ohio and Erie Canal reached Chillicothe, bringing with it canal-town prosperity. The Marietta and Cincinnati Railroad reached Chillicothe in 1852 and within a few years, after a bridge over the Ohio River was built at Belpre, the line became the Cincinnati, Washington & Baltimore. The Baltimore & Ohio Railroad Company bought the system in 1868. In most cases, having a railroad and a canal meant doom for the canal. In this case, however, the railroad ran east and west and the canal ran north and south. Thus, they complimented each other, making Chillicothe even stronger as it served as a port to both.

By 1875, the Cincinnati, Hamilton & Dayton Railroad and the Scioto Valley Railroad were also present. The canal survived until the flood of 1907. Chillicothe prospered further in 1917 when the U.S. government selected the area for a World War I army training site. In three months, 2,000 buildings were constructed and Camp Sherman was born. The town grew from a population of 16,000 to around 60,000 in just weeks, as the number of soldiers at the camp exceeded 40,000 at times. The aftermath of Camp Sherman is evident by a large Veterans Administration medical complex, three correctional complexes, and the Mound City National Monument—a Hopewell Culture burial ground, which probably would not have survived had the camp not occupied the site and made it part of a federal reservation.

Chillicothe continues to prosper with papermaking, Kenworth Trucks, dozens of smaller industries, and many tourist attractions. The historic downtown section, which dates back to the mid-1800s, is well preserved as a business district of shops and cafes.

1. "The Territory of the United States northwest of the river Ohio"—Congress passed the Ordinance of 1787 on July 13, 1787, defining the area of land covered by the ordinance.

One

THE VIRGINIA INFLUENCE

The first attempt to create a settlement in Virginia in 1606 failed. King James I of England speculated that too small a land area (some 200 miles square) may have been the reason. Therefore, when he wrote the charter of 1609, he specified a much larger area. The southern boundary was to go west to the South Sea (Pacific Ocean) and the northern boundary at a 45 degree angle up through Canada. After the Revolutionary War, the state of Virginia used the charter of 1609 to claim massive quantities of land to the west.

The following text labels appear on the map:

THE UNITED STATES
WHEN PEACE WAS DECLARED
in 1783
SHOWING THE STATE CLAIMS

Vermont had a state constitution and government but was not a member of the Confederation. Her soil was claimed by New York.

Western New York was claimed by Massachusetts. In 1786 a north line was drawn 82 miles west of the Delaware River and the land given to Massachusetts. The right to govern it remained with New York.

The western lands claimed by Massachusetts and Connecticut were also claimed by Virginia.

From the Lake of the Woods to the Mississippi River there was no boundary. The treaty said a west line from the Lake to the River, which was an impossible line.

Due to the land claims of some of the states, other states refused to ratify the new U.S. Constitution, thinking that the larger the land area, the more clout the bigger states would have. The federal government asked the states that were using the old charters to give up their claims for the common good of the new nation. The government wanted to sell some of this western land to development companies and use the money to pay back the states from which it had borrowed to support the Revolutionary War militia. Congress was trying to pay down the national debt. Most of the old claims were abandoned, and the Constitution was ratified. Also, in 1783, young Nathaniel Massie set out for what is now Kentucky with a land warrant for property located by Daniel Boone.

The Ordinance of 1787 established "The Territory of the United States northwest of the river Ohio" and named Marietta the capital. Arthur St. Clair was appointed the first governor. Connecticut retained some land along Lake Erie, which was known as the Western Reserve, and Virginia retained a 4.2-million-acre tract north of the Ohio River between the Little Miami and Scioto Rivers. Virginia planned to award the land to soldiers from Virginia who fought in the Revolutionary War, based on length of service and rank. This land was held free of federal government control until 1790, when all of the land warrants had been awarded. This opened the door for the sale of huge chunks of land for as little as 5¢ an acre. Massie, in Kentucky, and his friends and relatives, in Virginia, acquired thousands of acres in the Virginia Military District. Massie began locating and surveying land in the district in 1790. In 1793, he selected a site on which to found a settlement, but the Native Americans were not at peace. He returned in 1796 and founded Chillicothe on the banks of the Scioto River.

This map shows the outline of what became Ohio along with the various land districts. Note the vastness of the Virginia Military District and the location of Zanes Trace, extending from Wheeling to Limestone (Maysville), Kentucky. Nathaniel Massie picked the name Chillicothe based on the Shawnee word *Cheelakawtha*, meaning gathering place or town. Chillicothe and Zane's Trace were both started in 1796.

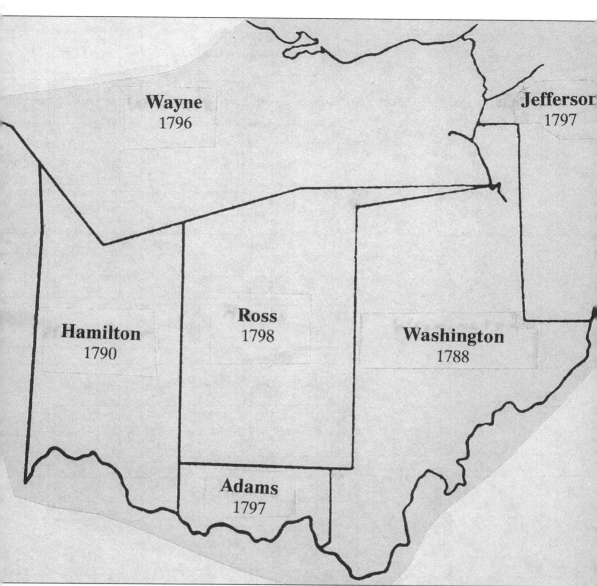

Wayne
1796

Jefferson
1797

Hamilton
1790

Ross
1798

Washington
1788

Adams
1797

Ross County was formed in 1798 as the sixth county in "The Territory of the United States northwest of the river Ohio." These original six counties have been divided and split so that today there are 88 counties in Ohio. The settlers in Ross County were mostly from Virginia and Kentucky, and were determined to build a new state—an idea much opposed by Gov. Arthur St. Clair in Marietta. The feud began and ran for five years. The Ordinance of 1787 specified that when 60,000 citizens of age over 21 were geographically grouped, that group could apply for statehood. St. Clair kept trying to split the territory east of Chillicothe in order to divide its population. In the end the people of Ross County won out and the territory was split to the west. Chillicothe was named capital of the Northwest Territory in 1800.

This map shows Chillicothe much the way Nathaniel Massie laid it out in 1796. Massie first stood at this site in 1793 and decided to make a settlement here. He saw the Scioto River to the north (the map is upside down compared to how we draw them today), hills to the west, Paint Creek to the south, and relatively flat and fertile land to the east to where the two streams met. He returned in 1795, but was run off by a band of hostile Shawnee. Massie promised an in-lot

14

and an out-lot to the first 100 settlers who agreed to stay for two years. In 1798, the two-year period was up and, at the same time, the County of Ross was formed with Chillicothe as the county seat. This made it easier to file the deeds of land transfers, most of which are still on file today in the Ross County Courthouse. Zane's Trace was also completed in 1798, bringing more settlers.

Thomas Worthington is considered the Father of Ohio Statehood. He, his brother-in-law Edward Tiffin, and their families moved from Virginia to Chillicothe in 1797. They brought with them their political views. Worthington bought land northwest of Chillicothe on which he planned to build a large stone home called Adena. He first built a large log house to live in while he collected the stone and timber required for the permanent home.

Edward Tiffin was married to Thomas Worthington's sister. Tiffin, Worthington, and Nathaniel Massie were elected to serve in the territorial legislature and were instrumental in getting a bill passed in Congress which split the territory on a line west of Chillicothe, creating the Indiana Territory and the Northwest Territory in 1800. Chillicothe was made the capital of the latter. When Ohio became a state in 1803, Tiffin became its first governor.

GOVERNOR EDWARD TIFFIN.

Two

STATEHOOD FOR OHIO IS BORN

Ohio's first state seal was conceived by William Creighton Jr. early one morning in 1802. Supposedly, several Chillicothians were meeting at Thomas Worthington's log home at Adena to discuss the details of statehood. At dawn they went outside just as the sun began to rise over the range of hills to the east, across the Scioto River valley. Wheat had been gathered into shocks in the valley, and the river was visible. Creighton designed the first seal in 1803, remembering that view. He also became Ohio's first secretary of state.

This is how Adena looked in 1903, after having been left by the Thomas Worthington descendants. Construction of the mansion was completed in 1808 by Worthington. It has been restored and is currently one Chillicothe's prize memorials, operated by the state.

This Jack Bennett sketch shows the old Ross County Courthouse and supporting structures before they were dismantled in 1852. The center building was used by the territorial legislature when Chillicothe was capital of the Northwest Territory and by the Ohio Legislature when Chillicothe was capital of the state. Ohio's Constitution was signed here in 1802. The *Chillicothe Gazette*, "the oldest newspaper west of the Alleghenies," built a likeness of the center stone building on West Main Street in 1940 and occupies it today.

Three

PAPERMAKING

Above is the Ingham Paper Mill as it appeared in 1876 on South Paint Street. Papermaking began in the Chillicothe area in 1810 and still exists today. The earlier efforts were north of town on the banks of Kinnikinnick Creek, near the Scioto River.

In 1837, a group of local businessmen used the waters of Paint Creek to build a canal, basin, and race system with a connection to the Ohio and Erie Canal. In 1847, David Crouse and William Ingham, who were making paper north of town, built a paper mill on South Paint Street to make use of the Hydraulic Canal system. Locating a paper mill at this location proved to be a godsend later. The Cincinnati, Hamilton & Dayton Railroad built its main line through the south side of town beside the paper mill, and in 1890, when Daniel Mead got off the train to find something to eat, he encountered a group of people at the mill attending an auction. Mead bought the paper mill for $24,900. Had food been served on trains in 1890, he would not have gotten off and Chillicothe would in all probability not have one of the largest Mead paper mills today.

19

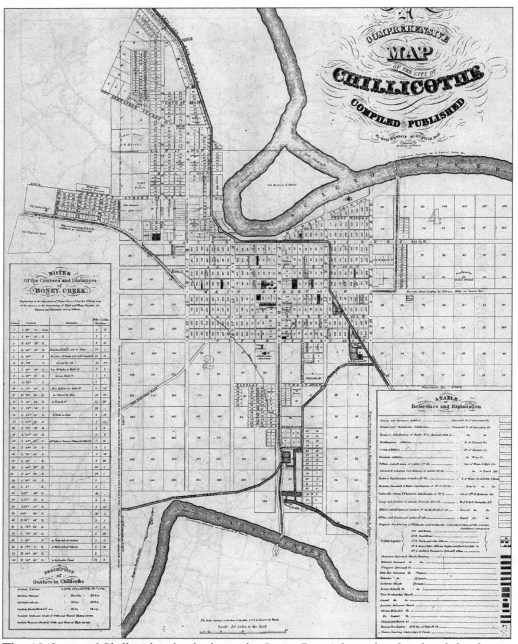

This 1843 map of Chillicothe clearly shows the Scioto River's horseshoe bend and the shorter channel that was created by floods in the early 1800s. The Marietta and Cincinnati Railroad later built its right-of-way across the heels of the horseshoe, trapping the river in the newer channel and leaving 48 acres of river bottom to be developed later into Yoctangee Park. The Ohio and Erie Canal enters town from the north, turns east along Water Street, and then south again. Paint Creek and the Hydraulic Canal can be seen at the bottom of the map, along with the Hydraulic Canal connection to the Ohio and Erie, near what is now Poland Park.

The Mead Paper Mill in 1900, just ten years after Daniel Mead bought it at auction. The Mead family entered the paper business in 1846 in Dayton, Ohio.

Daniel Mead invested heavily in the mill to update and expand it. This is how it looked in 1903. The mill got into financial trouble in 1905 and nearly closed, but some local bankers got together and pulled it through.

This 1907 view of the northern half of the Mead Paper complex shows the extent of expansion up to that time. George Mead had been brought in to manage the company.

This is the southern half of the Mead Paper complex in 1907. The Meads brought in paper machines from Dayton.

In 1920, construction of Mead's no. 2 mill began. This addition more than doubled the plant's manufacturing capability, bringing the total number of paper machines to nine.

Satisfying the need for pulpwood demanded a steady parade of pulpwood trucks, as seen here in 1929.

By 1940, Mead Paper included mills 1, 2, and 3, with a total of 11 paper machines. South Paint Street runs across in front of the complex, and most expansion is to the east.

In this northern view overlooking the eastern half of the city in the early 1950s, Mead has expanded so far as to be adjacent to the Chillicothe Paper Company, a separate company founded in 1919. In 1955, Mead Corporation bought the smaller company. Mead is the city's largest employer and has made Chillicothe "the white papermaking center of the world." The flat area across the Scioto River in the background shows the one-square-mile area once owned by Col. Ebenezer Zane, famous for Zane's Trace.

Four

OHIO AND ERIE
CANAL DAYS

This photograph taken in the 1890s shows the Marfield Mill (old Adams Mill) and the upper Marfield canal lock of the Ohio and Erie Canal. After the success of the Erie Canal in New York, the Ohio Legislature approved plans for two canal systems to run from Lake Erie to the Ohio River. Transporting goods by water was the most reasonable method, and Ohio needed to exploit its agricultural and manufacturing capabilities. The 308-mile-long (Cleveland to Portsmouth) Ohio and Erie Canal reached Chillicothe in 1831. Building such a canal presented many challenges. All built by hand, the Portage Lake System in Summit County and Buckeye Lake in Licking County were constructed as reservoirs for this canal. There were numerous state dams in many streams along the canal route to help maintain the water level. The Ohio and Erie Canal remained in use until the flood of 1907. North from the upper Marfield lock was the longest level section of the canal system: 17 miles to Circleville across two aqueducts, one at Yellowbud and the other across Deer Creek.

Marfield Locks Chillicothe Ohio.

This view shows both the upper and lower Marfield locks with state Route 104 to the right. These locks were used as swimming pools by soldiers at Camp Sherman during World War I, and later removed to Mound City and used to construct buildings. They are now part of Chillicothe's bicentennial walk-through monument in Yoctangee Park. Note the deterioration on the left of the lower lock.

A company called Brewer and Son got its start as a construction company by repairing canal structures such as the lower Marfield lock. Note the repair with brick and mortar. The waterfall device to the left was a regulator. Wooden planks could be added or removed to adjust the water level above the lock.

This early canal dredge worked the Ohio and Erie Canal at Frenchtown, just north of Chillicothe.

This powerhouse was across the canal from the end of Chestnut Street. Chillicothe's YMCA is now just north of this site, and the powerhouse is gone. Yoctangee Parkway is built over the canal bed.

The Ohio and Erie Canal turned eastward along Water Street at the head of Walnut Street. The Walnut Street footbridge was built in 1893. When the canal came through in 1831, the buildings facing the canal were 25 feet closer than those in this photograph, making Water Street extremely narrow. A fire in 1852 burned those buildings, and their replacements were built farther back and are still there today.

The flood of 1907 destroyed a nearby drydock and the Walnut Street footbridge. The levee holding the canal gave way and released the water into the old Scioto River bed in Yoctangee Park.

Looking west from the Paint Street bridge over the canal, this view shows the Walnut Street footbridge one block away. The Baltimore & Ohio Southwestern boxcar is on the spur used to haul coal to the old powerhouse (see page 27). Today, there are two B&O cabooses on this track used by the Ross-Chillicothe Convention and Visitors Bureau, and Water Street has been widened to cover the old canal bed.

This westward view shows Water Street canal frontage in the mid-1850s, before the Walnut Street footbridge was constructed. Imagine how narrow the street was when the previous buildings were 25 feet closer to the water's edge.

This winter scene shows Standard Elevator at Water and Paint Streets. The small, single-story part of the elevator nearest the viewer was originally the Marietta & Cincinnati passenger station. The conveyor was used to run corncobs down to the Juneman Electric Light Plant in the park. The Paint Street canal bridge rotated on a turnstile to allow boats through. The small single building was the bridge tender's shack.

When the canal went dry, boats were stranded wherever they happened to be. Pictured here is the canal boat *Duck* and its owner Faddy Swartz. Swartz lived on his boat along Water Street for years. At this site just west of Paint Street, the Sherman Theater was built in 1918.

The Ohio and Erie Canal continued east on Water Street to just past Mulberry Street. This 1903 view shows the canal turning south, with Standard Cereal Mill (not to be confused with Standard Elevator) in the background. The house behind the horse on the right is now a tanning salon.

The flood of 1907 drained the canal, as shown here at the same location as the above photograph. The railroads were well established by this time, so the state decided not to spend money to repair the canal. Canal lands were put up for lease by the state for several years and eventually were sold.

This winter scene, looking west up Water Street from just east of Mulberry Street, shows the Paint Street canal bridge one block away. The building on the extreme left is now a wallpaper outlet, and Water Street has been widened across the old canal bed into a boulevard.

The bridge tender shovels snow on the canal bridge at Mulberry and Water Streets. The bridge was at an angle so as to serve both streets. The sign warns of a $5 fine for allowing a horse to cross at faster than a walk. The bridge tender's shack is on the right.

The Second Street canal bridge was just east of Mulberry Street. The Machine Shop and Foundry on the left utilized a one-cylinder, natural gas engine with a huge flywheel to power overhead shafts which ran leather belts that drove a myriad of metal-working machines. The building on the right housed the Logan Car Company, one of Chillicothe's auto manufacturing plants.

The canal ran due south from Water Street to Main Street where it turned southeast into Sear's Basin. This northwest view shows the Sears Nichols Canning Factory on the extreme left and an old canal warehouse in the distance. The Main Street bridge over the canal was somewhat different from most because it held streetcar tracks. Today, this basin is a parking lot for a supermarket.

This lock at Fourth Street held back the water in Sear's Basin. The large wooden structure, built in 1833 as a flour mill, originally used canal water for power. The mill was converted to steam power c. 1890 and was destroyed by a fire in 1908. Note the lockkeeper's shack and the ramp to access canal boats.

The Fifth Street lock was the last lock in the city. This lock dropped the water to a basin in what is now Poland Park, near where the Hydraulic Canal terminated.

South of Chillicothe, the Ohio and Erie Canal crossed Paint Creek on this rickety looking aqueduct.

This photograph shows the same Paint Creek aqueduct in 1899, after undergoing some repairs and gaining a handrail. This aqueduct was destroyed during the 1913 flood.

This picture of the canal boat *E.L. Lybarger* was taken from the Lunbeck Road bridge *c.* 1896. The Scioto Valley Railroad is to the right and the Portsmouth Pike to the left. The buildings to the right were part of the Lunbeck Farm, which included a mill and a dam in Paint Creek. The road into Chillicothe required crossing a toll bridge over Paint Creek; so, during low water, some travelers elected to go through Lunbeck farm and ford Paint Creek to escape the toll.

The canal aqueduct over Paint Creek was washed out during the flood of 1913. This photograph shows some of the timbers from the aqueduct lodged on Lunbeck Dam.

Pete Malone's canal boat *Two Sisters* sunk in the canal just south of Chillicothe. Some parts of the canal held water for years after it was abandoned, especially after heavy rains.

The Scioto Valley Railroad, later the Norfolk & Western, had a bridge over the canal south of town. After the canal dried up, Ross County rerouted Three Locks Road to pass under this bridge, and in 1910, the N&W replaced the bridge with a larger one.

One of the structures built to supply water for the canal was this state dam south of Chillicothe. The dam was part of a system that included three adjacent canal locks. This dam provided water all the way south to Waverly, Ohio.

This old lithograph from an 1875 Ross County atlas shows the three locks and state dam. Three Locks Road is so named because it runs beside these locks. Chillicothe thrived as a canal town during the days of the Ohio and Erie Canal.

Five

RAILWAYS

The Marietta & Cincinnati Railroad appeared in Chillicothe in 1851. A bridge was built over the Ohio River at Belpre a few years later, and the railroad became the Cincinnati, Washington & Baltimore. Pictured above is a 2-6-0 Prairie-type locomotive of the CW&B. The Baltimore & Ohio Railroad Company bought the system in 1868, and the name B&O Southwestern or B&OSW came into being. As railroad traffic increased, the B&O made Chillicothe the division headquarters of the Ohio Division of the B&O, and Chillicothe became an important railroad center. In most cases the coming of a railroad meant the demise of the canal. However, in Chillicothe the railroad ran east and west and the canal ran north and south. Thus, they complimented each other and Chillicothe benefited by becoming a busy transfer point. In its heyday, the town had several freight trains and up to eight passenger trains passing through each day. When Camp Sherman appeared in 1917, the B&O had the only rail connection to it.

Shortly after the Baltimore & Ohio took control of the old Marietta & Cincinnati Railroad, improvements started. In 1870, the bridge over the Ohio and Erie Canal on the north side of town was replaced. In those days, bridge building included the construction of a wooden trestle to temporarily support the weight of the metal bridge and then the removal of the trestle when the bridge was finished.

As the 1870 Baltimore & Ohio Railroad bridge nears completion, new telegraph lines are run. In the distance to the left is the Chillicothe Wagon Company on Piatt Avenue. Note the curve of the canal as it nears Frenchtown to the right. When Camp Sherman was built in 1917, the military placed a storm sewer in the old canal bed, covered it over, and built the entrance road to the camp over the old bed. Part of this road still exists, but the railroad is gone.

Turnbuckles are tightened as a train runs across the new Baltimore & Ohio bridge over the Scioto River east of Chillicothe in 1877. The wooden Kilgore bridge in the background burned down the following year. Today, a steel bridge has replaced this B&O bridge and serves as a transfer line of the CSX (Chessie Transportation System).

B&O engine 1076, a 0-8-0 switcher with a slope-back tender, takes water by the sand house in Chillicothe in the 1880s. The dome on top of the boiler behind the bell held sand that was blown down on the rails for traction. All locomotives, even the diesels of today, do the same thing.

After the Scioto Valley Railroad came to town in 1875, Chillicothe Union Station was built to serve both lines where they crossed. Pictured here is a Baltimore & Ohio 4-4-2 Atlantic type, getting ready to leave with a westbound passenger train *c.* 1905. The Norfolk & Western took over the Scioto Valley line and added a second track in 1910, which meant the two tracks of the N&W crossed four of the B&O. This created quite a racket when trains were on the move.

The Baltimore & Ohio complex grew and grew, as shown in this photograph of 1896, the year that Chillicothe celebrated its centennial. Union Station is in the distance on the right.

The quick method of loading many tons of coal into the tender of a locomotive was with the use of a coal tipple. The tipple had compartments and a series of chutes, through which coal could be dumped in a hurry. The disadvantage was in getting the coal up the steep incline to the top, as seen in this photograph taken *c.* 1900.

This picture, taken from the top of the Baltimore & Ohio coal tipple, shows the Arbenz Furniture Factory, where the Arbenz Touring Cars were later manufactured, and the Florentine Pottery Works in the background.

Running tons of coal up and down many times a day tended to weaken wooden coal tipples, as with this one that collapsed in 1902.

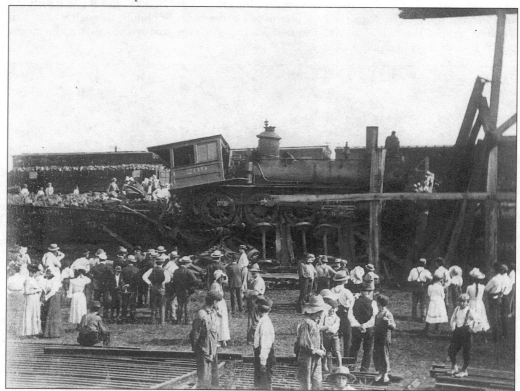

This is another view of the coal tipple collapse of 1902. One man was killed.

Being a main hub for a railroad meant that important people came to town on occasion, including presidential candidates such as Herbert Hoover, shown here at the Baltimore & Ohio complex in 1916.

Pres. Harry S. Truman campaigned in Chillicothe in 1952.

Chillicothe's Union Station was very active as the country went to war in the early 1940s. This view clearly shows the two tracks of the Norfolk & Western crossing the four tracks of the Baltimore & Ohio. Note the newsstand and the umbrella passenger sheds along the N&W tracks.

The EA-type passenger diesels were built for the Baltimore & Ohio in 1937. Here, no. 51 leads the National Limited through Chillicothe in the early 1940s.

The Cincinnati, Hamilton & Dayton Railroad built its line through the south side of town in the 1870s and had a passenger station on South Paint Street across from the paper mill. It was a train very much like the one pictured that Col. Daniel Mead left in search of food when he encountered the auction of the paper mill and bought it in 1890.

This was a rare photograph opportunity in 1913. The Baltimore & Ohio fill across the park had washed out during the 1913 flood (see page 64), and the Cincinnati, Hamilton & Dayton suffered similar damage. The B&O extended its spur from the old power plant in the background along the dry canal bed to Kopp Street to get around the washout until it could be replaced. Pictured above is a CH&D passenger train on B&O's temporary track, where Yoctangee Parkway is today in front of Chillicothe High School.

The Scioto Valley Railroad came through in 1875 but was soon taken over by the Norfolk & Western. This N&W Class K 4-8-2 is getting ready to leave for Portsmouth in 1945. The N&W built most of its own steam locomotives, including this one, in the company's shops in Roanoke, Virginia.

After years of using Norfolk & Western rails to get to Lake Erie, the Chesapeake and Ohio built its own right-of-way around Chillicothe in 1929. The C&O ran some pretty hefty steam power, such as this Texas Class 2-10-4, built in Lima, Ohio, in 1930. This photograph of no. 3002 was taken in 1932.

The Chillicothe Street Railroad Company dates back to 1876. Each car was pulled by a horse or a mule. Cars and animals were housed in the old horsecar barn on Church Street, as shown here *c.* 1891. The horsecar system presented many problems—derailments, animals quitting, and the "clean-up" after a day's work with the animals.

In the 1880s, all motive power was either horses or mules. Note the horse-drawn streetcar heading north on North Paint Street in front of the Ross County Courthouse.

The horsecar line was replaced with an electrified streetcar system in 1892. The streetcar barn and power plant was located at the northwest corner of Arch Street and Delano Avenue.

This is one of Chillicothe's early streetcars.

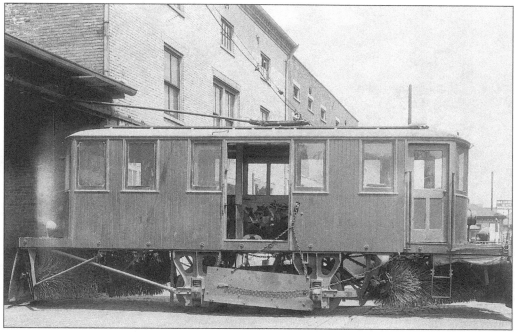

Pictured as it comes out of the old electric company garage on West Water Street is the system's snowplow and street cleaner.

A "bobber," or four-wheeled streetcar, turns north onto Paint Street from Main Street, c. 1909. Note the horses beside the no. 5 streetcar and the early automobile on the right. The mode of transportation was changing. Notice that there is a misspelled word in this photograph; it appears below the word "seeds."

The streetcar system was fully appreciated by the soldiers from Camp Sherman since the line ran right to the camp, making it easy to get to nearly anywhere in town. This camp-bound streetcar is pictured heading west on Second Street at Paint Street in 1918.

Chillicothe's last streetcar is shown making the turn at Paint and Main Streets on the last run on March 29, 1930. This brought to a close the city's history of street railway transportation.

In 1905, the Scioto Valley Traction Line was established to haul mail, milk, and passengers between Chillicothe and Columbus. The line required a bridge over the Scioto River next to the Bridge Street bridge. The two bridges became known as the Twin Bridges. At first, the traction line stopped at the end of the bridge, but it was extended later.

The bridges on Bridge Street looked so similar that on occasion, perhaps after a tour of the local taverns, motorists took the wrong bridge. This was not a good plan since the third rail had 1,100 volts in it. In town, the system used an overhead wire.

By 1908, the traction line had been extended to the head of Bridge Street at Main Street. Pictured above is car no. 108 getting ready to head north to Columbus. The fare was 25¢ each way. In 1911, a traction station was built on East Main Street, and the line was extended to form a loop around the station back to Bridge Street at Second Street.

The semaphore is down, signaling the traction car to stop for the lone passenger at the Hopetown stop. This car is southbound, meaning that the next stop is Chillicothe. Note the third rail with 1,100 volts—not a dog's best friend.

With the traction bridge over the Scioto River in the distance, this traction trestle extended northward over the river bottom. The Bridge Street highway bridge is visible at the extreme right.

The 1913 flood proved too much for the wooden traction trestle, and heavy repairs were required to restore service (see page 65).

The next traction line stop north of Hopetown was Kinnikinnick. To cross Kinnikinnick Creek, the line had a bridge under the Norfolk & Western railroad bridge. This 1910 view is looking south toward Chillicothe.

This view, looking north, shows the same bridges in 1910. State Route 180 crosses in the foreground. Note the Kinnikinnick traction stop on the left and the traction car approaching the Norfolk & Western bridge in the center. The Scioto Valley Traction Line ceased operation in 1930; no longer could anyone ride back and forth to Columbus for 25¢ each way.

Six

BRIDGES AND FLOODS

Bridges and floods have been grouped together in this book because, in most cases, bridges were the first to go in a flood. During the early 1800s, many attempts were made to raise money by lottery to build a bridge over the Scioto River at Chillicothe, and finally success was achieved. Built in 1817, the Bridge Street wooden toll bridge lasted until 1886 when it was torn down to be replaced. It is of interest to note that to the north of this bridge (left and away) is one square mile of land that once belonged to Col. Ebenezer Zane. When Zane petitioned Congress for his famous Zane's Trace back in 1796, he was to receive land near the river to support his ferry crossing. Land on this side of the river was in the Virginia Military District and was worth much more at the time than the congressional lands on the far side. Today, that square mile is Chillicothe's main shopping area (see page 24).

The plan was to tear down the wooden Bridge Street bridge and replace it with a modern iron bridge. As demolition proceeded, it became apparent that the old bridge was really well built, with 16-inch oak beams held together with wrought iron bolts. Note that in this 1886 photograph, the bridge had both a northbound and a southbound lane.

When demolition reached the point shown here, the decision was made to drill holes, fill them with kerosene, and burn the bridge down. It took several days for the superstructure to finally fall into the Scioto River.

The flood of 1898 was a major event in the history of Chillicothe. Pictured here is the Norfolk & Western railroad bridge over the Scioto River. To give the bridge ballast and to hold it in place, the train was taken out and left on the track. An armed guard kept people and looters away. The bridge was later replaced.

The east end of town suffered heavy damage during the flood of 1898. This picture shows Jackson School on the right. Mount Logan is in the background.

The East Main Street bridge system was made up of wooden spans, iron spans, and a causeway. The flood of 1898 washed out the westernmost span. This 1899 photograph shows the construction of an iron span to replace the missing span. Note the method of building: a wooden trestle supports the iron bridge until it is completed.

A temporary ferry was used in 1899 until the East Main Street bridge was back in service.

The South Paint Street wooden bridge over Paint Creek was a toll bridge. The original bridge at this site was burned in 1863 because the townspeople heard that Morgan's raiders were coming. Actually, Morgan's raiders never got within 40 miles of Chillicothe, and when the bridge was burned, the water in Paint Creek was only ankle deep.

This is a closer view of the South Paint Street bridge, taken from the north end. This bridge was replaced in 1911.

Note the temporary bridge on the far left in this 1911 construction photograph. The new bridge was made of concrete, which required wooden forms to create arches.

The finished concrete bridge with three arches is open to traffic.

When the Marietta & Cincinnati Railroad built its fill across the heels of the horseshoe bend of the Scioto River, a wooden trestle was installed at each end over the old riverbed. In later years as the fill was made higher by the Baltimore & Ohio, the old trestles were covered with rocks and dirt. This proved to be a mistake during the flood of 1907. As shown above, the easternmost part of the fill gave way, probably due to rotten timbers underneath.

The Baltimore & Ohio brought in a pile driver train from Cincinnati to repair the washout at the eastern end of the fill. When the train reached the western end of the fill where the other trestle had been covered, the fill gave way and dumped the train into the river. The center of the fill withstood the flood of 1907.

The entire fill was repaired and made higher after the flood of 1907, but it was not strong enough to withstand the flood of 1913. The Scioto River went on a rampage in March 1913. When the entire fill gave way in the middle of the night, it took only 20 minutes to completely fill the 48-acre Yoctangee Park and have water running down Paint Street.

Pictured here is the Pump House in Yoctangee Park during the flood of 1913. The Pump House was built, as its name implies, to pump water from the wells in the park to reservoirs on the hill. The Pump House survived and is today the Pump House Art Gallery. Inside at the top of the stairs is the watermark from the 1913 flood.

The flood of 1913 was the worst flood in Chillicothe's history. The iron Bridge Street bridge that replaced the old wooden bridge survived the 1913 flood as shown here.

The Scioto Valley traction bridge also survived the 1913 flood, but the wooden trestle on the right was severely damaged (see page 55).

Probably the most concentrated structural damage caused by the 1913 flood was on South Hickory Street. The levee at the head of Hickory Street gave way in the middle of the night and a wall of water raced south, washing away the street just south of Main Street, as shown above.

Hickory Street was completely destroyed from just south of Main Street all the way down to Fifth Street. The rushing water undermined the fronts of elegant brick homes on the west side of Hickory, causing the fronts to fall away, as seen here at the intersection of Fourth and Hickory Streets. Can you imagine being asleep, snug in your bed, when suddenly part of your bedroom disappears? There were several deaths caused by the flood of 1913, most of which were in the east end of town.

The last major flood to cause damage in Chillicothe occurred in January 1959. By that time North Bridge Street had been widened to four lanes and the old iron bridge had been replaced. North of the bridge, the roadway dropped down onto the floodplain. As shown here, the roadway was heavily damaged by the rushing water.

Pictured from Grandview Cemetery, the South Paint Street bridge over Paint Creek survives the 1959 flood (see page 61 for a drier view).

Many homes were damaged during the 1959 flood, as evidenced by this aerial view of the east end of town. Note Mount Logan School in the background.

East of Chillicothe, the Baltimore & Ohio right-of-way suffered a washout of two tracks and four switches in the flood of 1959. This is a westward view looking back toward town.

Seven

AROUND THE TOWN

Charles Foster is credited with making several sketches in and around Chillicothe in 1839, and this is one of them. The animals are grazing on an island in the horseshoe bend of the Scioto River, in what is now Yoctangee Park (see map on page 20). This portion of the river remains today as Yoctangee Park Lake. The Ohio and Erie Canal can be seen along West Water Street from just west of Paint Street to Walnut Street. All of the buildings along the canal were destroyed by the fire of 1852 and were rebuilt farther back from the canal to make Water Street wider.

A Charles Foster drawing shows how Paint Street looked in 1839 as viewed south from Water Street. The hill in the distance was later cut away to allow Paint Street to continue as a straight road all the way to Paint Creek, about a mile from this point.

This 1839 Charles Foster sketch shows the intersection of South Walnut Street (running off to the lower right) and West Fifth Street. The large building in the distance on the left was the Clinton House, which burned in the fire of 1852. The building with the pillars, to the right on Fifth Street, is today the McKell Library. The library and the museum in the building next door are owned and operated by the Ross County Historical Society. Four of the original Foster sketches are on display at the Ross County Historical Society's Museum.

This 1896 view of North Paint Street as seen from Water Street shows improvements made since the 1839 view on page 70. Note the streetcars turning the corner of Paint and Second Streets. The telephone lines on both sides of the street illustrate the competition between the Home Telephone Company on the left and the Bell Company on the right. Most businesses subscribed to both companies so that their customers would not have to pay the toll charges of calling from one company to the other.

The 73rd Regiment of the Ohio Volunteer Infantry had fought in Tennessee and were on furlough in Chillicothe before going to Gettysburg. Here, they are pose on Paint Street at the intersection of Second Street in January 1864. Note the canal in the background, the Paint Street footbridge, and beyond that, the railroad fill and Scioto River. The ruins on the right were left when the Madeira Hotel burned during the fire of 1852. All of the buildings on the right half of the photograph were built after the fire.

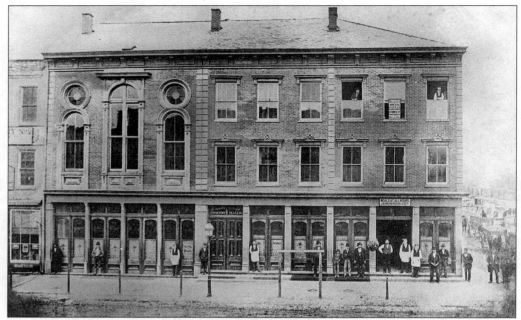

The Wissler Building faces east on Paint Street at Water. This photograph, taken *c.* 1875, shows the canal at the far right. During the days of Camp Sherman, the portion with the round windows was used as Officer's Club no. 1. The rack in front was used to dry fish.

In 1935, the *Scioto Gazette* was housed on the second floor in this building directly across the street from the Wissler Building. The Wagner's beer ad is on the side of the old Winter Garden which was built during World War I on the old canal land.

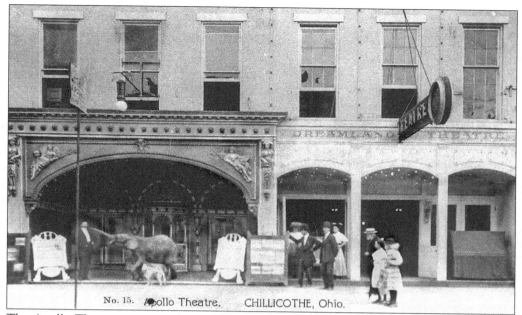

No. 15. Apollo Theatre.   CHILLICOTHE, Ohio.

The Apollo Theatre was next door to the Dreamland Theatre on North Paint Street, in this photograph from the early 1900s. Dreamland became the Star Theater in later years. Admission was 5¢.

C. Hartmeyer, family, and employees pose in front of the City Bakery on West Water Street. A bakery first opened at this location in 1806, and different families baked at this location until 1934.

The Knecht Brewery faced the Ohio and Erie Canal on East Water Street, as shown in this photograph taken *c.* 1905. Other owners brewed beer at this location well into the mid-1900s.

This is what East Second Street looked like as viewed from Paint Street, *c.* 1900. The Wissler Hardware Company had its horse-drawn delivery wagon backed up in front of the store, ready for loading. All of the buildings on the left were built after the fire of 1852.

The Ross County Bank building, pictured *c.* 1920, stood on the southwest corner of Paint and Second Streets for years until it was torn down to make room for Kresge's Department Store. Now Kresge's is gone, and the Law Enforcement Center occupies the location.

The Madeira Hotel stood on the northeast corner of Paint and Second Streets until the fire of 1852. The Nipgen building was constructed on this site in 1876.

The Lansing Block stands on the southeast corner of Paint and Second Streets. This 1876 view clearly shows the new horsecar tracks making the turn. Note the inside guardrail to help prevent derailments.

By 1906, the Wissler Hardware Company had upgraded its delivery service with a new Logan truck (compared with page 74). Logan automobiles and trucks were manufactured on East Second Street from 1903 to 1908 (see page 33). Wissler's truck was a one-cylinder, air-cooled, chain-driven vehicle with hard rubber tires.

The Masons rented the upper floor of a bank on East Second Street until the fire of 1852 destroyed the building. They bought the lot and built the Masonic Opera House in 1853. The building has been in use for entertainment ever since and is today the Majestic Theatre, used mostly for live stage shows. An electrified arch was moved here from Columbus in 1909 and still curves over the street in front of the theater.

East of the Masonic Opera House, about half the distance to Mulberry Street, was the Bonner Livery Stable. A fire in 1905 burned the livery to the ground. Firefighters were able to save adjacent buildings.

Fire Station no. 1 was moved from North Mulberry Street (see page 90) to this location on East Second Street in 1910. The move was five years too late to save the Bonner Livery Stable. The fire department is showing its wares in this 1910 photograph.

The Chillicothe Motorcycle Club lines up on Second Street just east of Fire Station no. 1 in 1912. At the time of this photograph, the building at the left was occupied by a heating and ventilating business. For many years, however, that building housed Fromm Printing, a well-known family of printers from Germany.

Believed to be the earliest photograph taken in Chillicothe, this daguerreotype shows the construction of the Union Block in 1848 on West Second Street. The Union Block and the building beside it are the only two structures in two entire city blocks that survived the 1852 fire. The top floors of both buildings were damaged, and today they are one story shorter. The building at the far right across Paint Street is the Madeira Hotel, which was lost in the fire. The original 1848 daguerreotype is owned by the Ross County Historical Society.

Near the time of World War I, David Meade Massie, a grandson of Chillicothe's founder Nathaniel Massie, stands in front of the First National Bank, of which he was president. The bank building is next to the Union Block on West Second Street.

Dan DeLong sits astride his 56-inch wheeler in front of his tire shop on North Walnut Street in 1933. DeLong sold bicycles and motorcycles as far back as 1913. He led nearly every local parade on one of his rare bikes, and he died of a heart attack during the Halloween Parade in 1956. This location is exactly where the fire of 1852 began. From this point the fire spread rapidly eastward for two city blocks.

Here on the southwest corner of Walnut and Water Streets, the original Clinton Hotel burned in the fire of 1852. The hotel was rebuilt, as can be seen in this 1907 photograph. Today this site is occupied by the Franklin Clinic.

This photograph c. 1895 shows the Hotel Carson on North Paint Street, next to the Ross County Courthouse. The Carson later became the McCarthy Hotel, and today the Law Enforcement Center is on this site.

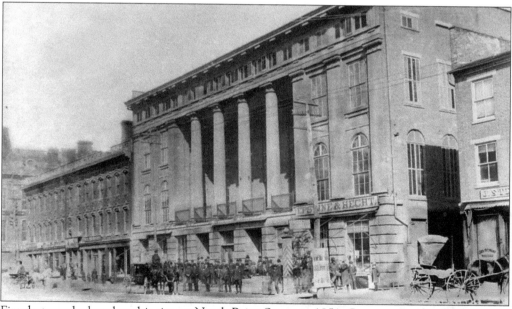

Fire destroyed a hotel at this site on North Paint Street in 1851. Construction began that same year to build a new hotel in its place, but completion was delayed until nearly 1855 because of the shortage of labor and material after the fire of 1852. The new hotel was called the Valley House and when ownership changed, it became the Emmitt House. Jake Warner remodeled it and renamed it the Warner Hotel c. 1886, after this photograph was taken.

The Warner Hotel on North Paint Street looked like this *c.* 1905. For years the hotel was a popular place. Today, the building houses offices, shops, and a restaurant in the front and apartments in the rear. Since the founding of the town, there has been some sort of lodging quarters on this site.

This view shows the east side of Paint Street, northward from Main Street. The Warner Hotel is on the left. The building on the right was torn down to make room for a new bank building in 1903. The street was paved with brick in 1898. This block of buildings is directly across from the Ross County Courthouse.

The Ross County Courthouse was built on the site previously occupied by the first Ohio statehouse. Pictured here in 1858, after two years of construction, the building still lacks a clock.

This photograph shows the Ross County Courthouse in 1886. The tower houses a clock with a black face and white numerals. Today the face of the clock is white with black numerals. Note the horsecar tracks at the intersection of Paint and Main Streets.

Pres. William Howard Taft came through Chillicothe on a campaign tour in 1912. Here, he is at the corner of Paint and Main Streets in the back of an Arbenz touring car. The car was manufactured in Chillicothe.

This is a 1907 picture of the Arbenz Furniture Factory on Washington Avenue in the east end of town. Note the Baltimore & Ohio coal tipple behind the building to the right. The Arbenz Motor Company was formed here in 1912 and built a few roadsters and touring cars. The effort was short-lived, and when the plant closed, the era of automobile manufacturing in Chillicothe ended.

The Hunn family ran a meat market on East Main Street for many years that was very successful. The market was just east of Hickory Street on the south side of Main Street.

This shows how Shines Restaurant looked at its grand opening in 1933. Located on East Main Street just east of Paint Street, the site has known many proprietors and is currently the location of a well-known pub called the Cross Keys Tavern.

Chillicothe's hook and ladder company poses in front of the old armory on West Main Street *c.* 1890. The building to the right is the Eastern Star Temple. Today, this is a parking lot.

The entrance to Grandview Cemetery used to be on South Walnut Street, as evidenced by this photograph *c.* 1890. Today, the entrance is on Belleview Avenue. Nathaniel Massie, Thomas Worthington, and other famous Ohio statesmen are buried at Grandview Cemetery.

This building on West Main Street was the headquarters of the *News Advertiser*, a newspaper that was in competition with the *Scioto Gazette*. The *Gazette* bought the *Advertiser* in 1938 and was ready to demolish this building when this photograph was taken. The *Gazette*, now named the *Chillicothe Gazette*, built a replica of the first statehouse as its headquarters on this site in 1940 and is still there. The *Gazette* is the "oldest newspaper west of the Alleghenies." The building to the left is the Eastern Star Temple.

On the south side of West Main Street near Walnut Street was the Bonner Brothers Furniture and Mantel Business, next to the New Nelson Hotel. The Bonners also ran a funeral service, which explains the presence of funeral hacks and carriages, c. 1895. The site of the Bonner building is now a parking lot.

The Chillicothe Public Library was built at 140 South Paint Street in 1906 and is still there today. The structure at the left was Central School, Chillicothe's first high school.

Pictured *c.* 1895 at 43 East Main Street is the Laycock Bicycle Depot and the Eichenlaub Bakery. This building is still in use.

In this photograph *c.* 1900, the Sears Nichols Canning Factory stood on the southeast corner of Mulberry and Main Streets. Sears Nichols canned just about anything a farmer could bring to town. The conveyor across Main Street was used to send cans to the canning factory. At the left is the approach to the East Main Street canal bridge and bridge tender's shack. Sear's Canal Basin (see page 33) is on the left side of the building. A supermarket now occupies the site.

Located on the northeast corner of Main and Hickory Streets was the Grove House. Built in 1814 as a cotton factory, Grove House was used as a meeting place for years. William Henry Harrison spoke here in 1840. Later, the Oil and Battery gas station stood here, and currently the Tabernacle Baptist Church occupies the corner.

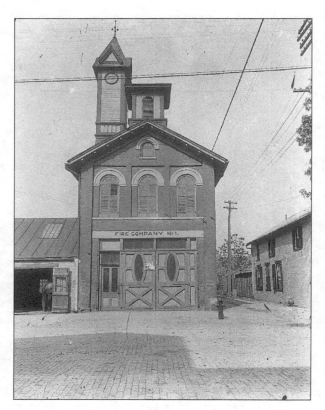

Fire Company no. 1 was on the west side of North Mulberry Street at the first alley. This building *c.* 1880 was used until the fire company moved to East Second Street in 1910 (see page 78). This photograph was taken shortly before the move.

This photograph shows Fire Company no. 1 at an earlier time, when horse-drawn fire engines were on display. Note the unpaved street.

Note the old carbide streetlight and the dirt road in this early photograph of a greenhouse on the northeast corner of Fourth and Watt Streets.

Pictured in 1911 on Cherry Street at Chestnut Street is Chillicothe's first building that was constructed as a hospital. Before this building was constructed, a house on North Bridge Street was used for a hospital.

The Wissler Brewery, shown here *c.* 1907, was located on Wissler Lane near the intersection of Main Street and Western Avenue. This brewery had a series of underground rooms for the storing and aging of beer. Hardly a trace remains today.

The Chillicothe Bottling Company faced Mill Street between Park Street and the old canal bed. For many years after this 1917 photograph was taken, countless bottles of milk and cola were bottled here.

Pictured in 1885, the old Carlisle Block was torn down to make room for a replacement. This building stood on the southeast corner of Paint and Main Streets.

The new Carlisle Building was constructed in 1885 on the site of the building in the photograph above. Note the skylight on the left, which was put there during construction to facilitate the Hathaway Studio. The Hathaway family relocated from Portsmouth to Chillicothe that year and are responsible for most of the images in this book.

This group of buildings on South Paint Street, extending from the Chillicothe Municipal Building on the left to within one building of the corner of Paint and Main Streets, was known as Commercial Row. The photograph is dated 1896, the same year the buildings were all torn down.

The Foulke Block was built in 1896 at the site of the old Commercial Row pictured above.

The Chillicothe Police Department, along with its ambulance patrol wagon, poses in front of the Chillicothe Municipal Building in 1910. The Foulke Block is on the right in this picture.

Across South Paint Street from the Foulke Block and next to the Carlisle Building is the Moser Building, shown here c. 1896. The Moser family was involved in many different kinds of businesses in the Chillicothe area for years. Here on Paint Street was the Moser Grocery.

Since Chillicothe is the birthplace of the state of Ohio, the Ohio centennial celebration of 1903 was a big event for the city. Here, Colonel Richard Enderlin leads the centennial parade southward on Paint Street past Fourth Street. Enderlin was a Civil War veteran.

A unit of the Ohio centennial parade passes along Paint Street at Fourth Street in 1903.

Part of the Ohio centennial celebration of 1903 took place in Yoctangee Park. This view is looking out of the park as people come and go. Part of the Paint Street canal bridge can be seen at left of center.

A lone Civil War cannon is on display in the park during the 1903 Ohio centennial celebration.

This is a view of the Civil War cannon in Yoctangee Park *c.* 1902. The park is still a very popular place to picnic, play, fish, walk, and feed the wild ducks and geese.

The National Guard Armory was built in the park behind the Civil War cannon in 1926.

Yoctangee Park Lake is a part of the riverbed of the old Scioto River that was salvaged as the park was being developed in the 1880s. An island in the river survived to be an island in the lake. This wooden footbridge allowed access to the island until being washed out in the flood of 1913.

Today, this little stone bridge, built in 1935, stands where the earlier wooden bridge stood.

Looking west at Yoctangee Park Lake *c.* 1900, the boathouse is on the left and the little gazebo on the right. To the left of the gazebo is the end of the island, and in the distance is the smokestack of the old powerhouse pictured on page 27.

This view is straight across the Yoctangee Park Lake, looking south at the boathouse. Behind the boathouse are the buildings along West Water Street that faced the canal. The canal was above, at the Water Street level. Barely visible above and a little to the left of the boathouse is a covered wagon.

Bicycling was the rage in the 1880s, and Yoctangee Park was a popular place for the sport. Members of the Chillicothe Bicycle Club pose with their high wheelers in the park in 1888.

Dr. W.A. Hall is credited with owning the first automobile in Chillicothe. Here, Hall poses in his 1901 Conrad in Yoctangee Park. The Conrad was shipped in pieces and had to be assembled locally. Benny Graham got the job of putting it together. Graham's interest in autos led him to build the Logans in later years.

Chillicothe is famous for an outdoor drama called *Tecumseh*, which is offered through the summer at an outdoor amphitheater just north of town. This photograph, taken in 1972, shows construction of the amphitheater. *Tecumseh* has been in continuous production ever since.

This photograph shows a scene of the first production of *Tecumseh*.

Eight

CAMP SHERMAN

When the United States entered World War I in 1917, the government sensed an immediate need for army training camps. Officials chose Chillicothe as a site for one of the camps. The government purchased land north of town, west of the Scioto River and as far east as the Baltimore & Ohio right-of-way. This photograph, looking east toward the Scioto, shows the valley that was designated for Camp Sherman, named for Gen. Wm. Telumseh Sherman of Civil War fame. The old Hopewell mounds are in the cornfield at the right, in front of the trees along the river. Surveyors came and started laying out the camp. The B&O built a switching spur, and construction got under way. Within three months, 2,000 buildings were completed and training began. The town grew from 16,000 to some 60,000 during the summer of 1917. In the fall of 1918, a Spanish flu epidemic hit the area, and 1,177 people died at the camp. The Majestic Theatre on East Second Street was used as a morgue, where bodies were piled like cordwood. It may be interesting to note that 1,177 men perished on the *Arizona* at Pearl Harbor on December 7, 1941, the same number that died of the flu at Camp Sherman. After the war, as the wooden buildings were being sold as surplus, the government saw the need for a permanent veterans hospital and built what is now the Veterans Administration Medical Center. Largely because of Camp Sherman, Chillicothe has the veterans hospital, two correctional facilities, Mound City, and hundreds of government-related jobs.

To support the construction of Camp Sherman, rail lines were extended, warehouses were erected, and supplies were shipped in. A distribution system of great magnitude was required.

Warehouse no.1 was just what the name implied. These are construction workers getting ready to set out on a days work of building a training camp in 1917.

The barracks constructed at Camp Sherman were two stories high. In just three months' time, 2,000 wooden buildings were completed. After the war the buildings were sold off as surplus, and many locals hauled the material away to build houses or additions to existing structures.

Building and operating a World War I training camp required the use of hundreds of horses and mules. Storage for their food and the care of the animals was a major undertaking.

These are new recruits arriving at Camp Sherman in 1917. The recruits came from all over the country, but mostly from cities and towns in Ohio. All of the streets at the camp were named for population centers in Ohio to help curb homesickness. Recruits from Toledo, Ohio, could walk down Toledo Avenue.

The recruits were fitted with uniforms that included boots and leggings. Sore feet produced a tired and irritable soldier.

This large brick farmhouse was once part of the Adams farm. It was used as the headquarters for Camp Sherman. When it was built in 1808, it faced toward the east. After the canal came through and roads were added to the west, additions to the house resulted in it facing west.

The only remaining wooden structure that was part of the original construction of Camp Sherman is the camp library building. This photograph shows the library in 1917. Local librarian Burton Stevenson set up the library system, ensuring a newspaper was available from every town represented by a soldier at the camp. Today, the library building is painted white, the skylight is covered, and there are roller doors along the sides. It is used by the government for equipment storage.

At the hub of the 11 buildings that made up the community group at Camp Sherman was the Community House. The largest of the 11 buildings, the Community House was used as an entertainment center for the soldiers. It burned to the ground in 1921. In the early 1930s, when the federal reformatory was built, a circular driveway was constructed over the roads entering the community group, from which some short streets ran to serve the houses built for prison employees.

This is the interior of the Community House as it appeared in 1917. A military band played at social events and dances. It was in vogue and very patriotic for ladies from Chillicothe to attend the dances.

The Knights of Columbus Hall was a very popular place to go and be entertained. There were many organizations represented at Camp Sherman, each with its own building. The YMCA had several sites.

The YWCA Hostess House was located in what is now the northeast corner of Mound City. The Hostess House was primarily for African-American soldiers, who were organized into separate units. Here, they relaxed, read, or entertained guests.

Of the three theaters at Camp Sherman, the Liberty was the largest. It was built primarily for the presentation of stage shows, and many were produced here. The Liberty Theatre burned down in 1921.

The Jewish Welfare Center, sponsored by the Jewish Welfare Board, welcomed all visitors regardless of their faith. The ditch in front of the center is all that was left of the Ohio and Erie Canal at that time.

The Salvation Army cabin was located in Frenchtown, adjacent to Camp Sherman. As shown in this 1917 photograph, the cabin was a popular place to go to and relax.

It was at Camp Sherman in 1917 that the first trench mortar battery was formed in the United States. Here, Lt. F.R. Rising gives instructions on implementation to: Sergeant Herz, Corporal Conlon, Corporal Halloway, E. Stengel, J. Baldwin, J. Will, C.S. Hoover, D.O. Jenkins, J. Reed, and Harry Cline.

When visitors came to Camp Sherman, some congestion resulted. The vehicular traffic is on today's state Route 104. The old canal bed is on the left, and the pedestrians are walking the old towpath of the canal. Through the trees in the distance on the right is the Main Camp Exchange, or PX.

In this rare photograph taken at Camp Sherman, the gentleman standing is General Glenn and seated to his right is Dwight D. Eisenhower.

One of two airplanes used at Camp Sherman for training was this Curtiss Jenny. The plane was used mostly to view exercises from above to detect flaws in the methods of training. This photograph was taken by one of the soldiers.

Some 200 German prisoners of war were held captive at Camp Sherman. This is the stockade that housed them. It appears to be one or more of the barracks that were fenced off with barbed wire. The prisoners were kept busy by farming a vegetable garden to help grow food for the camp. Having prisoners here during World War I might have given rise to the idea of building a reformatory at the site in later years.

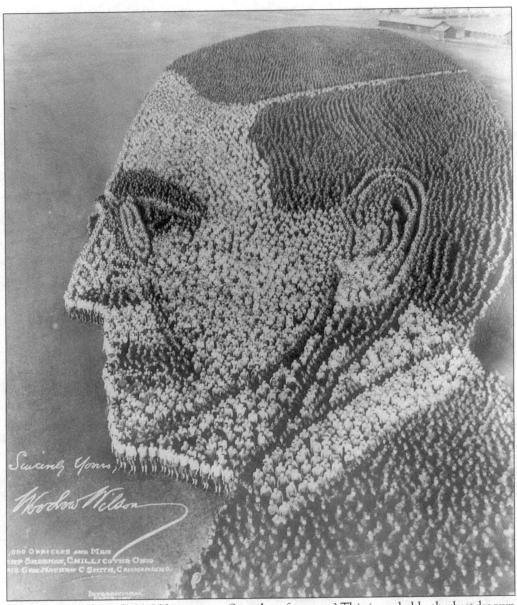

Sincerely Yours,

Woodrow Wilson

,000 Officers and Men
mp Sherman, Chillicothe Ohio
ig. Gen. Mathew C Smith, Commanding.

International

What can you do with 21,000 guys on a Saturday afternoon? This is probably the best-known photograph taken at Camp Sherman. A photographer named Arthur Mole visited several camps after the war to set up and record such scenes. He and an assistant laid out different colored cloth strips on the ground, erected a tower from which to photograph, and asked the commanding officer to order out the men dressed according to the strips on the ground. One soldier from Camp Sherman wrote home, "Dear Mom, Today I was part of President Wilson's left eyebrow." One interesting aspect of this particular photograph is the fact that when the sheriff of Ross County looked at it, he recognized someone who had escaped from his jail. The sheriff went to the camp, found the escapee, and escorted him back to jail. The aftermath of Camp Sherman left Chillicothe with a wealth of government resources. Today, there exists a veterans hospital, two correctional institutions, Mound City, and other support institutions.

Nine

CHURCHES

This section includes some of the earlier churches of Chillicothe. The one illustrated above is St. Paul's Episcopal Church at 33 East Main Street. It was built in 1833 and is still in use today. Pres. Bill Clinton visited Chillicothe in 1993, and while touring the city and seeing St. Paul's, he commented how he missed such old and preserved architecture back in Arkansas. The Civil War destroyed many of the South's older buildings.

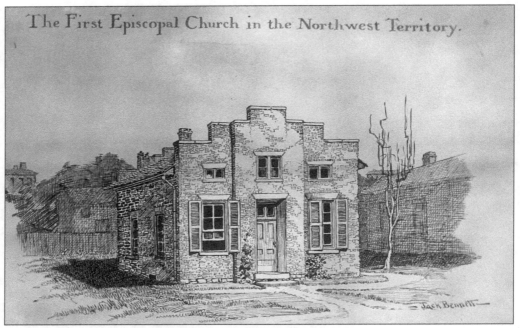

The First Episcopal Church in the Northwest Territory.

This is a sketch of the first Episcopal church in the Northwest Territory. The drawing is by Jack Bennett, and the church was on South Walnut Street. Built in 1821, the church was later used for private housing and was torn down in 1965.

The first Episcopal church was later converted into a multifamily residence. Today, this site is a parking lot for members of the Walnut Street Methodist Church.

The Methodists had a wooden church on West Second Street that burned down, so in 1850 they built this one on North Walnut Street. By 1905, they needed a new church and built one on the southwest corner of Main and Walnut Streets, a little less than a block away. The above building was used as an Eagles club for a long time and even had bowling alleys in it for a time. It was torn down in 1940.

The present Walnut Street Methodist Church, built in 1905, still stands at the southwest corner of Main and Walnut Streets. This photograph was taken in the late 1920s and shows the soldiers monument in the Main Street island, which stretched from Walnut Street to High Street. Col. Richard Enderlin had the monument created to recognize Chillicothe's veterans. The monument was moved to the park and placed next to the Armory in 1931 so that Main Street could be widened.

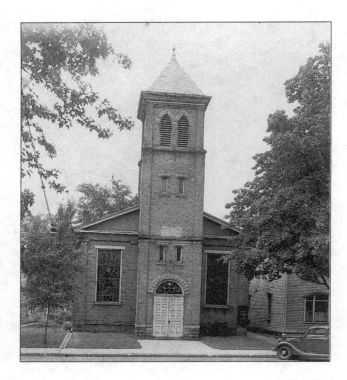

Built as St. John's Church in 1846, this church is in use today as Glorious Church of God in Christ. It is located at 123 West Main Street. The photograph dates from 1935.

The Presbyterians built a wooden church on West Main Street behind the old statehouse, but it burned down. In 1894, they built a church made of stone, and this is what it looked like when new, with the old Ross County Sheriff's Office on the right. In 1956, during an expansion at the rear, the stone church caught fire and was destroyed. The Presbyterians later built a new church on Belleview Hill, and a bank now occupies this site.

The First Baptist Church was built in 1865 and is still in use today at 65 West Fourth Street.

This photograph was taken in 1917 during the days of Camp Sherman. It is the soldier's rest room in the basement of the Presbyterian church on West Main Street (see facing page). Soldiers came here just to rest and read, or write letters home.

Trinity Methodist Church was erected on East Main Street just west of Mulberry Street in 1906. The site of the building at the left is now a courtyard and parking lot, but the church still remains today.

Salem Community Church at the northeast corner of Mulberry and Fourth Streets was rebuilt and expanded in 1910. The original building extends on the right toward Fourth Street, and the addition is on the left on Mulberry Street. On the inside the old and new sections blend as a whole.

The Quinn Chapel A.M.E. is located at 181 West Main Street. It was built in 1910 and is still in use today.

The Calvary Lutheran Church was built 1903. Located at 74 West Main Street, the church is still well attended.

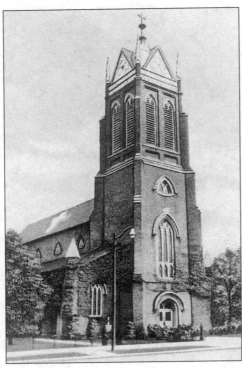

St. Mary's Catholic Church is located on South Paint Street, half way between Fourth and Fifth Streets. It was built in 1869 and is still in full operation today.

St. Peter's Catholic Church was built c. 1846. This photograph was taken c. 1918, before the church was remodeled. The remodeled church was destroyed by fire in 1947 and was replaced in 1949 by the current St. Peter's.

Ten

SCHOOLS

After the state of Ohio enacted the School Law, Chillicothe's first school board was established in 1849. The city clearly had a need for an organized system of education. The plan was to build three new school buildings: one in the east, one in the west, and one between the two. Pictured above c. 1890 from the Paint Street side is Central School, located on the northwest corner of Paint and Sixth Streets. The building was completed in 1853 and was used as Chillicothe's first high school, graduating three students in 1859. Western School was built in 1852 on the corner of Cherry and Chestnut Streets. The first Eastern School was also built in 1852 on East Main Street, near the Marietta & Cincinnati railroad right-of-way, which proved to be too dangerous as railroad traffic increased. By 1870, Eastern School had become overcrowded due to the growth in the east end of town. Thus, it was replaced by a new Eastern School on the west side of Bridge Street between Main and Second Streets. Southern School was built on the corner of Walnut and Seventh Streets in the mid-1870s. It was intended to be used by African-American students. Over time, new schools were built and old ones were torn down. By 1999, the Chillicothe school system included five elementary schools, two middle schools, and one high school. Chillicothe High School has occupied no fewer than four sites.

The West Fifth Street School was built as a new high school in 1901. High school classes were conducted here until another high school was constructed on Arch Street in 1932, the same year the West Fifth Street School became West Fifth Street Junior High School. This building was torn down in 1974 to make room for a new Central Elementary School.

This was the new Chillicothe High School on Arch Street. The Class of 1933 was the first to graduate from this school, and the Class of 1962 was the last. Another new school was built as the high school on Yoctangee Parkway, from which the Class of 1963 graduated. The building pictured above became Smith Middle School in 1963 and still is.

The original Western School was built in 1852, but it was torn down in 1911 to make room for the Western School seen here. It was used as an elementary school until 1951. Today, it is used mainly by the board of education for administrative purposes and occasionally for classrooms in time of overcrowding.

The second Central School, Central Elementary, was completed in 1916 on the site of the first Central School (see page 123). This building stood until another Central Elementary School was constructed on West Fifth Street, where West Fifth Junior High had been. Today, this site serves as a school playground and a parking lot for the library next door.

Southern School, on the corner of Walnut and Seventh Streets, was used mainly by African-American students from 1874 to 1956. The building was razed shortly after 1956, and the site is now a public park. Some members of Chillicothe's African-American community regretted that the building was not saved and used as a museum dedicated to their culture.

The second Eastern School replaced the first one in 1870. This building along with its school yard was a city block long, running from Main Street to Second Street on the west side of Bridge Street. The fire escapes were the school's most unique feature. Notice the vertical black tubular structure on the right between the trees. Inside the tube was a spiral slide that allowed people on the top two floors to make a hasty exit. The site was abandoned as a school in 1951. A gas station, a motel, and a McDonald's restaurant occupy the site today.

Mount Logan School faced East Main Street at Douglas Avenue where the trolley tracks ended. Built in 1927, the school was used for grades one through eight. In 1974, a new middle school and an elementary school replaced it. Some of the students of Mount Logan were rumored to have greased the trolley tracks so that the streetcar would slide off the tracks and down the brick street. The conductor always carried a broom to help get the trolley back on the overhead wire.

This is how St. Mary's Catholic School looked when it first opened on East Fourth Street in 1912. It was used as a parochial school for the Catholic community for years. The upper grades were known as Catholic Central High School or CCHS as opposed to CHS for Chillicothe High School. The building was torn down in 1994 to make room for a modern fellowship center.

ACKNOWLEDGMENTS

It is impossible to give credit to all of those who contributed in some way or another to the making of this book. Special credit must be given to those who created the images used herein: William Creighton Jr., who sketched the first state seal; artists H.H. Bennett, Jack Bennett, and Charles Foster, who were "the eyes of a camera" before the camera was invented; the Hathaway family photographers, who photographed in Chillicothe from 1885 through 1953 and whose images are reprinted here from original negatives; photographers F.C. Mader, Albert Scholl, Arthur Mole, Charles Schlegel, Mrs. Krick, Charles Tomastik, Joe Vickers, John Grabb, F.A. Simonds, Jim Beavers, Burton Stevenson, soldiers at Camp Sherman, and countless others who take pictures just for the fun of it. Some of the images come from privately owned scrapbooks assembled by Floyd Brown, Rosemary Yager, Charles Alexander, and Bill Grady.

A special credit must be given to the Ross County Historical Society, who owns the originals of most of the sketches and copies of photographs seen in this publication. Without the Society's preservation of our heritage, many facts and images would be forever lost.

Also, thanks go to the Ohio Historical Society, who has played a major role in the restoration and preservation of Worthington's home; Adena, which is open to the public as a state memorial; and the Hopewell National Historic Park, or Mound City, which is maintained by the National Park Service. Thanks also must be extended to the publishers of old history books, from which some of the old maps and illustrations have come; the Chillicothe Bicentennial Commission; and the Chillicothe Bicentennial Publications Committee, which published a record of historical details, used to substantiate some of the dates and spellings in this publication.

This book is dedicated to my patient wife, Susie.

Visit us at
arcadiapublishing.com

CPSIA information can be obtained
at www.ICGtesting.com
Printed in the USA
LVHW06*1349170618
580992LV00017B/179/P